THE GOLDEN-MOUTHED

THE GOLDEN-MOUTHED

*Selected Poetry of
Vladimir Mayakovsky
and Boris Pastermak*

Translated from Russian by
Andrey Kneller

Copyright ©2004

All rights reserved. Printed in the United States of America. No part of this publication may be reproduced, stored in a retrieval system, or transmitted, in any form or by any means electronic, mechanical, photocopying, recording, or otherwise, without the prior written permission of the author.

ISBN 1-58961-160-8

Published by PageFree Publishing, Inc.
733 Howard Street
Otsego, MI 49078
www.pagefreepublishing.com

CONTENTS

Introduction 7
A Note on Translation 11

VLADIMIR MAYAKOVSKY

About Petersburg 17
Listen! 18
A Violin and a Little Nervous 20
Lilichka! 23
Moonlit Night 26
To His Own Beloved Self the Author Dedicates
   These Lines 27
Spring 30
Kindness to Horses 31
Attitude to a Lady 34
Heine-Imitation 35
She loves me… 36
Past One O'clock… 37
A Cloud in Trousers 38
Backbone Flute 74
I Love 89

BORIS PASTERNAK

February 109
Venice 111
After the Interlude 113
Nobel Prize 115
Peerless Days 117

THE POETRY OF DR. ZHIVAGO

Hamlet 121
March 123
Easter 125
White Night 128
Spring Floods 131
Confession 134
Summer in the City 136
The Wind 138
Hop 139
Indian Summer 140
Autumn 142
Fairytale 144
August 150
Winter Night 153
Parting 155
Meeting 158
Sunrise 161
Earth 163
Bad Days 166
Magdalene I 168
Magdalene II 170
The Garden at Gethsemane 173
Acknowledgements 177

INTRODUCTION

"... if I place Pasternak and Mayakovsky side by side, — place side by side, and not present them together, — it is not because one isn't enough or one needs the other, or completes the other; I repeat; each is full to the brink, and Russia is full to the brink with each one of them, and not only Russia, but poetry itself, — I do this to represent twice what, God willing, happens once in half-a-century: here, natures offers it twice in half-a-decade: the complete and full wonder of a poet."

—Marina Tsvetaeva
From "Epos and Lyric"

In Russia, Vladimir Mayakovsky and Boris Pasternak have long been acclaimed as the two of the greatest poets of the twentieth century. In the West, however, their poetry is yet to be fully discovered. I hope that this collection of poetry will shed some light on the true nature of their talents.

Time and time again, Vladimir Mayakovsky has been portrayed as *"The Poet of the Revolution,"* a headstrong communist, who wrote propaganda in support of the Communist Party and praised the struggles of working class against the wealthy. In reality, that is a rather one-sided portrait of the poet who completely bent the boundaries of language and introduced an entirely different style of poetry. His irregular line-breaks, his use of internal rhyme, his control of meter and his sense of rhythm combined together to form his unique style. His imagery is overflowing with allusions, metaphors and hyperboles. His major works, "A Cloud in Trousers," "Backbone Flute," and "I Love," sparkle with wit, wisdom and originality. To fully enjoy and understand Vladimir Mayakovsky's work one has to set aside the context and focus on the text alone. His lyrical love poetry deserves to be recognized and praised for its breath-taking beauty.

Boris Pasternak became known in the West after he was awarded the 1958 Nobel Laureate in Literature and was forced by the Russian authorities to decline the prize. This scandal won him a large audience in the West and his novel, Dr. Zhivago became an instant success. However, contrary to popular belief, Boris Pasternak never rebelled against the Soviet regime. His poetry always reflected his inner self and was never dictated by the atmosphere of the epoch. In Russia, where the novel, <u>Dr. Zhivago,</u> had been banned until the late 1980's, Boris Pasternak was primarily known for his work as a poet. One could, indeed, enjoy his poetry without even noticing the historic background. Boris Pasternak, whose first true love was music, brings a unique sense of melody to his poetry. Barely a whisper, one almost needs to overhear the subtle song in his words. It is this quality of his poetry that sets him apart from his contemporaries and makes his work moving and unforgettable.

A NOTE ON TRANSLATION

Conventionally, translators focus on literal translations and pay extra close attention to word choice, often disregarding the rhythm and/or rhyme of the original piece. While this works for most other languages, Russian poetry is very melodic and it is precisely its rhythm that makes it so distinct. Take for example Vladimir Mayakovsky's "A Violin and A Little Nervous." He makes the whole poem weep like a nervous violin with irregular line-breaks, rhymes and repetition:

> *The violin was panicking, imploring*
> *and suddenly burst into tears,*
> *so child-like and pesky*
> *that the drum couldn't stand it:*
> *"All right, all right, all right!"*

Reading the poem, you cannot help but feel that you're in the audience listening to the polyphony of violins, helicons and cymbals. Likewise, in the poem, "The Wind," Boris Pasternak creates almost a haunting sense of reality, as if the reader is actually standing outside and watching the tree trunks bending with the *"whimpering"* winds:

> *The wind is whimpering and sobbing.*
> *It rocks the forest and the cabin.*
> *At once all of the tree trunks bending...*

All of this is created through the careful application of alliteration, assonance, rhythm and rhyme. Both, Boris Pasternak and Vladimir Mayakovsky use this skill to make their poems come alive in the mind of the reader. I've tried my best to render this into English without sacrificing the content of the poem. At times, even my best efforts proved to be unsatisfactory and some of my favorite poetry had to be left out. Precisely for this reason, the poems "Wedding," "Star of Nativity," and "The Miracle," from Dr. Zhivago do not appear in this collection. After numerous attempts at translating these poems, I felt that I could not do them justice in the English language.

The translations that appear in this book are based on Vladimir Mayakovsky: Collected Works in Eight Volumes, published in Moscow, Russia by

"Pravda" in 1963 and <u>Boris Pasternak: Collected Works in Two Volumes</u>, published in Tula, Russia by "Filin" in 1994.

VLADIMIR MAYAKOVSKY

ABOUT PETERSBURG

From rooftops, tears seeped into pipes
and to the river's arm drew streaks,
while lips, suspended from the skies,
continued sucking on stone teats.

The sky, relaxed, could now see clearly:
where shines the sea's resplendent channel,
the sweating cameleer drove wearily
The Neva's[1] lazy, two-humped camel.

1913

---

[1] **Neva**: A river flowing through St. Petersburg, connecting Lake Ladoga with the Gulf of Finland, an inlet of the Baltic Sea.

LISTEN!

Listen!
if the stars are lit,
then someone must need them, of course?
then someone must want them to be there,
calling those droplets of spittle pearls?

And wheezing,
in the blizzards of midday dust,
he rushes to God,
fearing he's out of time
and sobbing,
he kisses God's sinewy hands,
tells Him that it's important,
pleads to Him that the star must shine!
vowing
that he won't survive the starless torment!
And later,
he rambles, worried,
though seemingly calm and fit,

and tells somebody:
"Finally, nothing can
frighten you,
right?!"
Listen!
if the stars are lit,
then someone must really need them?
then it is essential
that at least one star
alights
over the rooftops each night?!

1914

A VIOLIN AND A LITTLE NERVOUS

The violin was panicking, imploring
and suddenly burst into tears,
so child-like and pesky
that the drum couldn't stand it:
"All right, all right, all right!"
It got wearied, couldn't wait till the violin finished,
slipped out onto the gleaming Kuznetsky[2]
and took flight.
The curious orchestra looked on as
the violin wept itself out,
without words
or cadence
and only the nearby seated,
foolish cymbals

---

[2] **Kuznetsky Most**: one of Moscow's most fashionable streets.

kept banging:
"What is it?
Who did it?"
And when the helicon,
brass-faced
and covered with sweat,
shouted:
"Stupid,
crybaby,
get some sense!"
across the notes,
I staggered ahead
over the horror-struck music stands.
For some reason, I cried out:
"Goodness!"
and its long, wooden neck I embraced:
"Violin, we are similar
don't you see that?
I also
shout a lot
and like you, I can't prove my case!"
The musicians laugh at me:
"He's been caught
by a wooden girl, what could be better?!
That genius!"
But I don't care what they say
I'm a good guy...
Hey, violin, you know what?

Let's
live together!
eh?

1914

LILICHKA!

(Instead of a letter)

Tobacco smoke eats the air away.
The room,—
a chapter from Kruchenykh's[3] Inferno.
Recall,—
by the window,
that day,
I caressed you ecstatically, with fervor.
Here you sit now,
with your heart in iron armor.
In a day,
you'll scold me perhaps
and tell me to leave.
Frenzied, the trembling arm in a gloomy parlor
will hardly be able to fit the sleeve.

---

[3] **A. Kruchenykh:** (1886-1970) a contemporary poet of Vladimir Mayakovsky, one of the leaders of the futurism movement.

I'll rush out
and hurl my body into the street,—
distraught,
lashed by despair and sadness.
There's no need for this,
my darling,
my sweet.
Let's part tonight and end this madness.
Either way,
my love is
an arduous weight,
hanging on you
wherever you flee.
Let me bellow out in the final complaint
all of my heartbroken misery.
A laboring bull, if he had enough,
will leave
and find cool water to lie in.
But for me,
there's no sea
except for your love,—
from which even tears won't earn me some quiet.
If an elephant wants to relax, he'll lie,
pompous, outside in the sun-baked dune,
Except for your love,
there's no sun
in the sky
and I don't even know where you are and with whom.

The Golden-mouthed

If you thus tormented another poet,
he
would trade in his love for money and fame.
But
nothing sounds as precious to me
as the ringing sound of your darling name.
I won't drink poison,
or jump to demise,
or pull the trigger to take my own life.[4]
Except for your eyes,
no blade can control me, no sharpened knife.
Tomorrow you'll forget
that it was I who crowned you,
who burned out the blossoming soul with love
and the days will form a whirling carnival
that will ruffle my manuscripts and lift them above...
Will the dry autumn leaves of my sentences
cause you to pause,
breathing hard?

Let me pave a path with the final tenderness
for your footsteps as you depart.

1916

---

[4] "**...take my own life...**": Vladimir Mayakovsky did take his own life when he shot himself in his Moscow apartment on April 14, 1930.

MOONLIT NIGHT

The moon is emerging.
It going to be here
soon.
And now, it hangs in the air, full and stark.
That is probably God,
with a divine
silver spoon,
groping in the fish-soup of stars.

1916

TO HIS OWN BELOVED SELF THE AUTHOR DEDICATES THESE LINES

Six.
As heavy as a blow.
"Render unto God… render unto Caesar…"[5]
But where is someone
like me
to go?
What refuge or shelter is there?

---

[5] **Render Unto God:** See Matt. 22:15-22; Mark 12:13-17; or Luke 20:20-26

If only I were
shallow,
like the Pacific Ocean,—
I'd rise on the tiptoes of waves
to caress the moon with the tide.
Where shall I find a beloved
of my proportions?
She'd never fit into the miniature sky!
Oh, if only I were poor!
like a millionaire!
What's cash for the soul?—
a thief driven by greed.
The gold of all californias, I swear,
isn't enough for the ravenous hordes of my needs.
Oh, if only I were tongue-tied
like Dante[6]
or Petrarch![7]
I'd ignite my soul for a single love!
and with poetry, I'd set her ablaze!
If my words
and my love
were a triumphal arch:
the inamoratas of all the ages,
would pass through it gallantly, leaving no trace.

---

[6] **D. Alighieri**: (1265-1321) the author of the Divine Comedy, one of the greatest of literary classics.
[7] **F. Petrarca** (1304-1374) an Italian poet and humanist, one of the great figures of Italian literature.

The Golden-mouthed

Oh, if only I were
quiet,
like thunder,—
I'd moan
and the earth would tremble, languished.
If I
allow my vast voice
to rumble,—
the comets, wringing their burning arms,
would plunge in anguish.
I would gnaw the nights with the rays of eyes,—
if I were
as dim as the sun,
I'd shine!
Why should I feed
the earth's scrawny bosom
with my brilliant, radiant light?!
I shall go on,
dragging behind me my love's huge clod.
In that remarkable night,—
delirious, feverish and haunted,—
by what Goliaths[8] was I begot,
so enormous
and so unwanted?

1916

---

[8] **Goliath:** in the Bible, a giant of Gath, who challenged the Israelites.

SPRING

The city drops the wintry features.
The snow-banks release their saliva.
Again, the spring has reached us,
like a cadet, — foolish and lively.

1918

KINDNESS TO HORSES

The hooves stomped faster,
singing as they trod:
—Grip.
Grab.
Rob.
Grub.

Wind-fostered,
ice-shod,
the street skidded.
Onto its side, a horse
toppled,
and immediately,
the loafers gathered,

as crowds of trousers assembled up close
on the Kuznetsky,[9]
and laughter snickered and spluttered.
—"A horse tumbled!"
—"It tumbled — that horse!"
The Kuznetsky cackled,
and only I
did not mix my voice with the hooting.
I came up
and looked into
the horse's eye...
The street, up-turned,
continued moving.
I came up and saw
tears, — huge and passionate,
rolling down the face,
vanishing in its coat...

and some kind of a universal,
animal anguish
spilled out of me
and splashing, it flowed.
"Horse, there's no need for this!
Horse, listen,—
look at them,—
do you think that you have it worse?

---

[9] **Kuznetsky**: (see note 2 on page 20).

The Golden-mouthed

Child,
we are all, to some extent, horses,—
everyone here is a bit of a horse."
Perhaps
she was old
and didn't want to be nursed,
or maybe, she took in my speech with a scoff,
but
the horse,
out of nowhere, suddenly burst,
heaved to its feet,
and neighing,
walked off.
Wiggling its tail,
with its mane shinning gold,
it returned to the stall,
full of jovial feelings
and imagined once more
that it was a colt,
and work was worth doing
and life was worth living.

1918

ATTITUDE TO A LADY

This evening was to decide
were we to fall in love passionately?—
it's dark,
no one would see us.
I leaned over her actually,
and actually,
while
I was leaning,
I said to her
like a kind father :
"Emotions are steep like cliffs,—
please,
step away farther.
Farther,
step away, please."

1920

HEINE-IMITATION[10]

Lightning streaked out of her eye:
"I saw you
with another lady.
You're the most heartless,
the most horrible guy..."
and went on,
and went on,
and went on, blaming.
Listen, I'm an educated chap, darling,
let's just end it right there, don't grumble.
If I wasn't killed by the lightning,
then, I swear,
I'm not scared of the thunder.

1920

---

[10] **H. Heine:** (1797-1856), a German romantic poet.

SHE LOVES ME...

She loves me? Not? I twist my arms like I'm crazy
and having broken my fingers,
                              fling them away.
It is thus that the petals of the first-found daisies
are plucked, and guessed on,
                              and sent off in May.
I won't hide the grayness the razor reveals.
Let the ringing silver of the ages commence.
But I pray that I never regain in these years
the disgraceful and shameful common sense.

1928-1930

PAST ONE O'CLOCK...

Past one o'clock. You're probably in bed.
The Milky Way streams like the silver Oka.[11]
I won't send wild telegrams. I don't intend
to trouble you and vex you any longer.
And now, as people say, our case is closed.
The boat of love could not endure the grind.
We're even now. And there is no remorse,
let's not bring up the sorrows left behind.
Behold what hush has fallen on the ground!
The starry night is grandiose and spacious.
At times as these, you rise and speak aloud
to ages, histories and all creation.

1930

---

[11] **Oka**: A river in the western Russia.

A CLOUD IN TROUSERS

Prologue

Your thought,
Fantasizing on a sodden brain,
Like a bloated lackey on a greasy couch sprawling,—
With my heart's bloody tatters, I'll mock it again.
Until I'm contempt, I'll be ruthless and galling.

There's no grandfatherly fondness in me,
There are no gray hairs in my soul!
Shaking the world with my voice and grinning,
I pass you by, — handsome,
Twentytwoyearold.

Gentle souls!
You play your love on the violin.
The crude ones beat it out on the drums violently.
But can you turn yourselves inside out, like me,
And become just two lips entirely?

Come and learn,—
You, decorous bureaucrats of angelic leagues!
Step out of those cambric drawing-rooms

And you, who can leaf your lips
Like a cook leafs the pages of her recipe books.

If you wish,—
I'll rage on raw meat like a vandal
Or change into hues that the sunrise arouses,
If you wish,—
I can be irreproachably gentle,
Not a man, — but a cloud in trousers.

I refuse to believe in Nice[12] blossoming!
I will glorify you regardless,—
Men, crumpled like bed-sheets in hospitals,
And women, battered like overused proverbs.

---

[12] **Nice:** a city on the French Riviera, a popular tourist destination, famous for its flower market.

Part I

You think I'm delirious with malaria?

This happened.
In Odessa, this happened.

"I'll come at four," promised Maria.[13]

Eight...
Nine...
Ten.

Soon after,
The evening,
Frowning,
And Decemberish,[14]
Left the windows
And vanished in dire darkness.

Behind me, I hear the neighing and laughter
Of candelabras.

---

[13] **Maria:** refers to a girl that Vladimir Mayakovsky had met while he was in Odessa. The "Maria" in Part IV is quite another person.
[14] **Decemberish:** One of the trademarks of Vladimir Mayakovsky's poetry is that he often made up his own words that would gain their meaning in the context of the poem. This is a good example.

The Golden-mouthed

You wouldn't recognize me if you knew me prior:
A bulk of sinews
Moaning,
Fidgeting.
What can such a clod desire?
But the clod desires many things.
Because for oneself it doesn't matter
Whether you're cast of copper
Or whether the heart is cold metal.
At night, you want to wrap your clamor
In something feminine,
Gentle.

And thus,
Enormous,
I hunch in the frame,
And with my forehead, I melt the window glass.
Will this love be tremendous or lame?
Will it sustain or pass?
A big one wouldn't fit a body like this:
It must be a little love, — a baby, sort of,
It shies away when the cars honk and hiss,
But adores the bells on the horse-tram.
I come face to face
With the rippling rain,
Yet once more,
And wait
Splashed by the city surf's thundering roar.

Running amok with a knife outside,
The night caught up to him
And stabbed him,
Unseen.

The stroke of midnight
Fell like a head from a guillotine.

The silver raindrops on the windowpane
Were piling a grimace
And yelling.
It was as if the gargoyles of Notre Dame
Started yelping.

Damn you!
Haven't you had enough yet?
Cries will soon cut my throat all around.

I heard:
Softly,
Like a patient out of his bed,
A nerve leapt
Down.
At first,
He barely moved.
Then, apprehensive
And distinct,
He started prancing.

The Golden-mouthed

And now, he and another two,
Darted about, step-dancing.

On the ground floor, the plaster was falling fast.

Nerves,
Big ones,
Little ones,—
Various!—
Galloped madly
Until, at last,
Their legs wouldn't carry them.

The night oozed through the room and sank.
Stuck in slime, the eye couldn't slither out of it.
Suddenly, the doors started to bang
As if the hotel's teeth were chattering.

You entered,
Abrupt like "Take it!"[15]
Mauling the suede gloves you carried,
And said:
"You know,—
I'm soon getting married."

---

[15] **Take it**: A title of one of Mayakovsky's poems.

Get married then.
It's all right,
I can handle it.
As you can see, I'm calm, of course!
Like the pulse
Of a corpse.

Remember?
You used to say:
"Jack London,[16]
Money,
Love and ardor,"—
I saw one thing only:
You were La Gioconda,[17]
Which had to be stolen!

And someone stole you.

Again in love, I shall start gambling,
With the fire illuminating the arch of my eyebrows.
And why not?
Sometimes, the homeless ramblers
Will seek to find shelter in a burnt down house!

---

[16] **J. London:** (1876-1916) one of the most successful American writers of the early 20th century.
[17] **La Gioconda**: Leonardo da Vinci's "Mona Lisa", was stolen from the Louvre in 1911.

The Golden-mouthed

You're mocking me?
"You've fewer emeralds of madness
than a beggar kopecks, there's no disproving this!"
But remember
Pompeii[18] came to end thus
When somebody teased Vesuvius!

Hey!
Gentlemen!
You care for
Sacrilege,
Crime
And war.
But have you seen
The frightening terror
Of my face
When
It's
Perfectly calm?

And I feel-
"I"
Is too small to fit me.
Someone inside me is getting smothered.

---

[18] **Pompeii:** An ancient Italian city, located near Naples and at the foot of Mt. Vesuvius. The eruption of Vesuvius in 79 A.D. buried the city under cinders and ashes.

The Golden-mouthed

Hello!
Who's speaking?
Mother?
Mother!
Your son has a wonderful sickness!
Mother!
His heart has been set alight!
Tell Lydia and Olga, his sisters,
That there's simply no where to hide.
Every word,
Whether funny or crude,
That he spews from his scorching mouth,
Jumps like a naked prostitute
From a burning brothel.

People sniff—
Something's burned down.
They call the firemen.
In glittering helmets,
They carelessly start intruding.
Hey, tell the firemen:
No boots allowed!
With a sizzling heart one has to be prudent.
I'll do it!
I'll pump my watery eyes into containers.
Just let me push off my ribs and I'll start.

I'll leap out! I'll leap out! You can't restrain me!
They've collapsed.
You can't leap out of the heart!

From the cracks of the lips,
A cindering kiss springs,
Running away from the smoldering face.

Mother!
I can't sing.
In the heart's chapel, the choir was set ablaze!

The figurines of words and numbers
From the skull,
Like kids from a burning building, scurry.
Thus fear,
Reaching up to the sky, called
And raised
Lusitania's[19] fiery arms with worry.

A hundred-eyed blaze looked into the peace
Of apartments, where the people perspired.
With a final outcry,
Will you moan at least,
To report to the centuries that I'm on fire?

---

[19] **Lusitania:** liner under British registration, sunk off the Irish coast by a German submarine on May 7, 1915. The incident contributed largely to the rise of American sentiment for the entry of the United States into World War I.

Part II

Glorify me!
The great ones are no match for me!
Upon everything that's been done
I stamp the word "naught."
As of now, I have no desire to read.
Novels?
So what!

This is how books are made,
I used to think,—
Along comes a poet,
And opens his lips with ease.
Inspired, the fool simply begins to sing,—
Oh please!
It turns out:
Before they can sing with elation,
On their calloused feet they tramp for some time,
While the brainless fishes of imagination
Are splashing and wallowing in the heart's slime.
And while, hissing with rhymes, they boil
All the loves and the nightingales in a broth-like liquid,
The tongueless street merely squirms and coils,—
It has nothing to yell or even speak with.

In our pride, we work all day with goodwill
And the city towers of Babel[20] are again restored.
But God
Grinds
These cites into empty fields,
Stirring the word.

In silence, the street dragged on the ordeal.
A scream stood erect on the gullet's road.
While fat taxies and cabs were bristling still,
Wedged in the throat.
As if from consumption,
The trodden chest gasped for air.

The city, with gloom, blocked the road rather fast.

And when,—
Nevertheless! —
The street coughed up the strain onto the square
And pushed the portico off its throat, at last,
It seemed as if,
Accompanied by the choirs of an archangel's chorus,
Recently robbed, God would show us His heat!

---

[20] **Babel**: in the Bible, place where Noah's descendants (who spoke one language) tried to build a tower reaching up to heaven to make a name for themselves. For this presumption the speech of the builders was confused, thus ending the project.

But the street squatted down and yelled out coarsely:
"Let's go eat!"

The Krupps[21] and the Krupplets gather around
To paint menacing brows on the city,
While in the gorge,
Corpses of words are scatted about,—
Two live and thrive,—
"Swine"
And another one,—
I believe, "borsch".

And poets, soaking in sobs and complaining,
Run from the street, resentful and sour:
"With those two words there's no way to portray now
A beautiful lady,
Or love
Or a dew-covered flower."

And after the poets,
Thousands of others stampeded:
Students,
Prostitutes,
Salesmen.

---

[21] **Krupps:** the German munitions-makers.

The Golden-mouthed

Gentlemen,
Stop!
You are not the needy;
How dare you to beg them, gentlemen!

Covering yards with each stride,
We are healthy and ardent!
Don't listen to them, but thrash them instead!
Them,
Who are stuck like a free add-on
To each king-size bed!

Are we to ask them humbly:
"Help us, please!"
Imploring them for hymns
And oratorios?
We are the creators with the burning hymns
To the hum of the mills and laboratories.

Why should I care about Faust?
In a fairy display of the fireworks' loot,
He's gliding with Mephistopheles on the parquet of galaxies!

I know,—
A nail in my boot
Is more frightening than Goethe's[22] fantasies!

I am
The most golden-mouthed,[23]
With every word I am giving
The body a name-day,
And the soul a rebirth,
I assure you:
The minutest speck of the living
Is worth more than I can ever do on this earth!

Listen!
The present-day Zarathustra,[24]
Wet with sweat,
Is dashing among you and preaching here.
We,
With faces crumpled like a bed spread,
With lips sagging like a chandelier,
We,
The Leprous City detainees,

---

[22] **J.W. von Goethe** (1749-1832) A German poet, dramatist, novelist, and scientist.
Faust: the hero of Goethe's poetic drama of the same name.
Mephistopheles: The name of the devil in the legend of Faust.
[23] **Golden-mouthed:** This expression was used to describe articulate and expressive preachers in the Russian Orthodox Church.
[24] **Zarathustra:** c.628 BC-c.551 BC, religious teacher and prophet of ancient Persia, founder of Zoroastrianism.

The Golden-mouthed

Where, from filth and gold, lepers' sores were raised,
We are purer than the Venetian azure seas,
Washed by the sunshine's balmy rays.

I spit on the fact
That Homer and Ovid didn't create
Soot-covered with pox,
Men like us all,
But at the same time, I know
That the sun would fade
If it looked at the golden fields of our souls.

Muscles are surer than prayers to us!
We won't pray for aid any more!
We—
Each one of us—
Holds in his grasp
The driving reins of the world!

This led to Golgotha in the auditoriums[25]
Of Petrograd, Moscow, Kiev, Odessa,
And there wasn't one of you
Who wasn't imploring thus:
"Crucify him!"
Teach him a lesson!"
But to me,—

---

[25] **"This led to my Golgotha in the auditoriums..."** Here, Mayakovsky alludes to his travels around Russian at the end of the year 1913, when his presentations were harshly criticized and bashed by the press.

People,
Even those of you who were mean,—
To me, you are dear and I love you with passion.

Haven't you seen
A dog licking the hand that it's being thrashed by?

I am laughed at
By the present-day tribe.
They've made
A scabrous joke out of me.
But I can see crossing the mountains of time,
Him, whom the others can't see.

Where men's sight falls short,
Wearing the revolution's thorny crown,
Leading at the head of the hungry horde,
The year 1916 is coming around.

Among you, his precursor,[26]
Wherever there's pain, I'll be near.
I have nailed myself to the cross there
On every single drop of a tear.
There's nothing left to pardon now!
In souls that bred pity, I burnt out the fields.
That is much harder than
Taking a thousand thousands of Bastilles.

---

[26] **His precursor:** An allusion to St. John the Baptist.

And when
His advent announcing,
Joyful and proud,
You'll step up to greet the savior,—
I will drag
My soul outside,
And trample it
Until it spreads out!
And give it to you, red in blood, as a flag.

Part III

Ah, how and wherefrom
Did it come to this
That the dirty fists of madness,
Against the luminous joy, were raised in the air?

She came,—
The thought of a madhouse
And curtained my head with despair.

And
As in the Dreadnought's[27] downfall
With chocking spasms
The men jumped into the hatch, before the ship died,

---

[27] **Dreadnought**: a heavily armed battleship whose main guns are all of the same caliber.

The crazed Burlyuk[28] crawled on, passing
Through the screaming gaps of his eye.
Almost bloodying his eyelids,
He emerged on his knees,
Stood up and walked
And in the passionate mood,
With tenderness, unexpected from one so obese,
He simply said:
"Good!"[29]

It's good when from scrutiny a yellow sweater[30]
Hides the soul!
It's good when
On the gibbet, in the face of terror,
You shout:
"Drink Cocoa — Van Houten!"[31]

This moment,
Like a Bengal light,
Crackling from the blast,

---

[28] **D. Burlyuk:** (1887-1967) A painter, a poet, one of the leaders of the futurist movement and a close friend of Vladimir Mayakovsky. Burlyuk was blind in one eye.
[29] **"Good":** the title of one of Vladimir Mayakovsky's poems.
[30] **Yellow sweater:** Vladimir Mayakovsky's famous futurist garb.
[31] **"Drink Cocoa — Van Houten!"** According to the story that was covered by the media at the time, before the his execution, a man yelled out the commercial slogan, "Drink Cocoa- Van Gouten!" For this advertisement, the company Van Houten promised a large sum of money to support the man's family.

The Golden-mouthed

I wouldn't exchange for anything,
Not for any money.

Clouded by cigar smoke,
And stretching like a liquor glass,
One could make out the drunken face of Severyanin.[32]

How dare you call yourself a poet
And gray, like a quail, twitter away your soul!
When
With brass knuckles
This very moment
You have to split the world's skull!

You,
With one thought alone in your head,
"Am I dancing with style?"
Look how happy I am
Instead,
I,—
A pimp and a fraud all the while.

From all of you,
Who soaked in love for plain fun,

---

[32] **I. Severyanin:** (1887-1941) A contemporary poet of Mayakovsky, considered cheap and superfluous by his colleagues because he was given to lauding the wealth and luxury of the high life in his poetry.

Who spilled
Tears into centuries while you cried,
I'll walk away
And place the monocle of the sun
Into my gaping, wide-open eye.

I'll wear colorful clothes, the most outlandish,
And roam the earth
To please and scorch the public,
And in front of me,
On a metal leash,
Napoleon will run like a little puppy.

Like a woman, quivering, the earth will lie down,
Wanting to give in, she will slowly slump.
Objects will come alive
And from all around,
Their lips will lisp:
"Yum-yum-yum-yum-yum!"

Suddenly,
The clouds
And other stuff in the air
Stirred in some astonishing commotion,
As if the workers in white, up there,
Declared a strike, all bitter and emotional.

The Golden-mouthed

The savage thunder peeked out of the cloud, irate.
Snorting with huge nostrils, it howled
And for a moment, the face of the sky bent out of shape,
Resembling the iron Bismarck's[33] scowl.

And someone,
Entangled in the clouds' maze,
To the café, stretched out his hand now:
Both, tender somehow,
And with a womanly face,
And at once, like a firing cannon.

You think
That's the sun above the attics,
Gently stretching to caress the cheeks of the café?
No, advancing again to slaughter the radicals
It's General Galliffet![34]

Take your hands out of your pockets, wanderers.
Pick up a bomb, a knife or a stone
And if one happens to be armless,
Let him come to fight with his forehead alone!

---

[33] **O. von Bismarck:** (1815–98) A German statesman, known as the Iron Chancellor.
[34] **G. de Galliffet:** (1830-1909) A French General, whose cruel suppression of the Commune of Paris in 1871 won him a reputation as a strong man and the enduring enmity of the political left.

Go on, starving,
Servile
And abused ones,
In this flea-swarming filth, do not rot!

Go on!
We'll turn Mondays and Tuesdays
Into holidays, painting them with blood!
Remind the earth whom it tried to debase!
With your knives be rough!
The earth
Has grown fat like the mistress' face,
Whom Rothschild[35] had over-loved!

May the flags flutter in the line of fire
As they do on holidays, with a flare!
Hey, street-lamps, raise the traitors up higher,
Let their carcasses hang in the air.

I cursed,
Stabbed
And hit in the face,
Crawled after somebody,
Biting into their ribs.

---

[35] **Rothschild:** A famous banking family, known for their wealth.

In the sky, red like La Marseillaise,[36]
The sunset gasped with its shuddering lips.

It's insanity!

Not a thing will remain from the war.

The night will come,
Bite into you
And swallow you stale.

Look,—
Is the sky playing Judas once more,
With a handful of stars that were soaked in betrayal?

The night,
Like Mamai,[37] feasted with delight,
Crushing the city with its bottom's heft.
Our eyes won't be able break through this night,
As black as Azef![38]

---

[36] **La Marseillaise:** the song of the French Revolution, the French National Anthem.

[37] **Mamai:** Khan of the Golden Horde at the end of the fourteenth century, during the Tartar domination of Russia. In reality, it wasn't Mamai, but the warlords of Jenghiz Khan era, who practiced the ritual of feasting while sitting on wooden boards placed on the bodies of the prisoners.

[38] **E. Azef: (1869-1918)** The notorious *agent provocateur* who played a double game, engineering the assignations of imperial ministers and betraying revolutionaries to the czarist police.

Slumped in the corner of the saloon, I sit,
Spilling wine on my soul and the floor,
And I see:
In the corner, round eyes are lit
And with them, Madonna bites the heart's core.

Why bestow such radiance on this drunken mass?
What do they have to offer?
Can't you see, once again,
They prefer Barabbas[39]
Over the Man of Golgotha?

Maybe, deliberately,
In the human mash, not once
Do I wear a fresh-looking face.
I am,
Perhaps,
The handsomest of your sons
In the whole human race.

---

[39] **Barabbas:** A bandit held in jail at the time of Jesus' arrest. Pontius Pilate, who, according to the Gospels, annually released a prisoner at Passover, offered to release Jesus, but the people demanded his death and Barabbas' delivery.

The Golden-mouthed

Give them,
The ones molded with delight,
A quick death already,
So that their children may grow up right;
Boys — into fathers
Girls — into pregnant ladies.

Like the wise men, let the new born babes
Grow gray with insight and thought
And they'll come
To baptize the infants with names
Of the poems I wrote.

I praise the machine and the industrial Britain.
In some ordinary, common gospel,
It may perhaps, be written
That I'm the thirteenth apostle.[40]

And when my voice bawdily rumbles,
Every evening,
For hours and hours,
awaiting my call,
Jesus, Himself, may be sniffling
The forget-me-nots of my soul.

---

[40] **Thirteenth Apostle:** The original title of the poem, rejected by the czarist censors.

Part IV

Maria! Maria![41]
Let me in, Maria!
Don't leave me out on the street!
You can't?
My cheeks cave in,
But you wait ruthlessly.
Soon, sampled by everyone,
Stale and pallid,
I'll come out
And mumble toothlessly
That today I'm
"Remarkably candid."

Maria,
You see,—
My shoulders are drooping again.

In the streets, the men
Prick the fat in their four-story craws.
They show their eyes,
Worn out in the forty years of despair, and restless.
They snicker because
In my teeth,
Again,
I hold the hardened crust of last night's caresses.

---
[41] **Maria:** A Moscow painter and a writer with whom Mayakovsky was involved at the time.

The Golden-mouthed

The rain wept over the sidewalks,—
That puddle-imprisoned fraudster.
The corpse of the street, clobbered by cobbles,
soaked in its cries.
But the gray lashes,—
Yes! —
The eyelashes of icicles became frosted
With tears from the eyes,—
Yes! —
From the drainpipe's overcast eyes.

Every pedestrian was licked by the rain's snout:
Athletes glistened in the carriages on the street.
People burst
Overstuffed,
And their fat oozed out,
Like a muddy river, it streamed on the ground,
Together with juices from
A cud of old meat.

Maria!
How can I fit a tender word into bulging ears?
A bird
Sings for alms
With a hungry voice
Rather well,

But I am a man,
Maria,
Coughed up by the ailing night into Presnya's[42] filthy palms.

Maria, do you want me?
Maria, take me in, please.
With shivering fingers I'll squeeze the iron throat of the bell!

Maria!

The pastures of streets turn wild and loud!
They're squeezing my neck and I'm almost collapsing.

Open!

I'm hurt!

Look,— my eyes are pricked out
By the common womanly hatpins!

You've opened the door.
My child!
Oh, don't be alarmed!

---

[42] **Presnya:** A street (and a district) in Moscow where Mayakovsky lived.

The Golden-mouthed

You see these women,
Hanging on my neck like mountains, —
Through life, I drag with me
A million of massive, enormous, pure loves
And a million millions of filthy, disgusting lovelets.
Don't be afraid
If betraying the vow
Of honesty,
Seeing a thousand pretty faces, I'll throw myself at them, —
"Those, who love Mayakovsky!"-
Please, understand that that is the destiny
Of the queens, who have mounted the heart of a madman.

Maria, closer!

Whether naked and shameless,
Or shivering in dismay,
Yield the wonder of your lips, so gentle:
My heart and I have never lived until May,
But in my past,
A hundreds of Aprils assembled.

Maria!
A poet sings praises to Tiana[43] all day,

---

[43] **Tiana:** A character in the poem by I. Severyanin. (see note 32 on page 57).

But I,—
I'm made of flesh,
I'm a man,—
I ask for your body,
Like the Christians pray:
"Give us this day
Our daily bread."

Maria, give it to me!

Maria!
I fear to forget your name
As a poet fears to forget under pressure
A word
He conceived in a restless night,
Equal to God in effect.

Your body
I shall continue to love and treasure
As a soldier
Amputated by war,
Alone
And unwanted,
Cherishes his remaining leg.

Maria,—
You won't have me?
You won't!

The Golden-mouthed

Ha!

Then gloomy and dismal,
Once more,
I shall carry
My tear-stained heart
Forward,
Like a dog,
Limping,
Carries the paw
That the speeding train had ran over.

With the blood from the heart I cheer the road that I roam,
Flowers cling to my jacket, making it dusty,
The sun will dance a thousand times round the earth,
Like Salome[44]
Danced around the head of the Baptist.

And when my years, at their very end,
Will finish their dance and wrinkle,
A million bloodstains will spread
The path to my Father's kingdom.

---

[44] **Salome:** In the New Testament, she is the daughter of Herod Philip and Herodias, who danced to obtain the head of John the Baptist.

I'll climb out
Filthy (sleeping in gullies all night),
And into his ear, I'll whisper
While I stand
At his side:

"Mister God, listen!
Isn't it tedious
To dip your generous eyes into clouds
Every day, every evening?
Let's, instead,
Start a festive merry-go-round
On the tree of knowledge of good and evil!
Omnipresent, you'll be all around us!
From the wine, all the fun will ensue
And Apostle Peter, who's always been frowning,
Will perform the fast-paced dance, ki-ka-pu.[45]
We'll bring all the Eves back into Eden:
Order me
And I'll go,—
From the boulevards, I'll pick up all the pretty girls needed
And bring them to you!

Should I?

---

[45] **Ki-ka-pu:** An exotic dance that was popular at the Russian night clubs at the time.

The Golden-mouthed

No?

You're shaking your curly head coarsely?
You're knitting your brows like you're rough?
Do you think
That this
Winged one, close by,
Knows the true meaning of love?

I too am an angel; used to be one before,—
With a sugar lamb's eye, I stared at your faces,
But I don't want to give presents to mares anymore,—
All the torture of Sevres that's been made into vases.[46]
Almighty, You created two hands,
And with care,
Made a head, and went down the list,—
But why did you make it
So that it pained
When one had to kiss, kiss, kiss?!

---

[46] **"All the torture of Sevres…":** Vases from the well known factory in Sevre, France.

I thought that you were the Great God, Almighty,
But you're a miniature idol, — a dunce in a suit,
Bending over, I'm already reaching
For the knife that I'm hiding
At the top of my boot.

You, swindlers with wings,
Huddle in fright!
Ruffle your shuddering feathers, rascals!
You, reeking of incense, I'll open you wide,
From here all the way to Alaska.

Let me go!

You can't stop me!
Whether I'm right or wrong
Makes no difference,
I will not be calmer.
Look,—
The stars were beheaded all night long
And the sky is again bloody with slaughter.

Hey you,
Heaven!
Take your hat off,
When you see me near!

The Golden-mouthed

Silence.

The universe sleeps.
Placing its paw
Under the black, star-infested ear.

1914-1915

BACKBONE FLUTE

Prologue

For all of you,
Whom I've admired or still am admiring,
Hidden like icons in the cave of the soul,
Like a goblet of wine at a festive gathering,
I shall raise my heavy, verse-brimming skull.

More and more often, I wonder,—
Why shouldn't I place
The period of a bullet at the end of my stanza?[47]
Today,
Just in case,
I am giving my final, farewell concert.

---

[47] **Period of a bullet:** (see note 4 on page 25).

The Golden-mouthed

Memory!
Gather into the brain's auditorium
The bottomless lines of those who are dear to me.
From eye to eye, pour mirth into all of them.
Light up the night with the by-gone festivity.
From body to body, pour the joyous mood.
Let no man forget this night.
Listen to me, I will play the flute.
On my backbone tonight.

I

I crumble miles of streets with extended strides.
Bearing this hell, where can I stray thus?!
What heavenly Hoffman[48] alone at night
Thought of your likeness, accursed and heinous?!

The streets are too narrow for the joyful storm.
The dressed up people disperse, enthralled.
I ponder.
Like blood clots, sticky and warm,
My thoughts are slithering out of my skull.

---

[48] **E.T. A. Hoffmann**: (1776-1822) A German writer, composer, and painter. He is well known for his short stories in which supernatural characters reveal people's hidden secrets.

I,
The creator of all that's festive and mirthful,
Always go to the feast on my own, alone.
Watch me now as I jump down, doleful,
And splatter my head on the Nevsky[49] stones!
I blasphemed,
I swore and denied God's existence,
But God pulled such a woman out of the infernal bowel
That the mountains trembled seeing her in the distance.
He brought her to me and commanded:
Love her!

God is content.
On a crag,[50] under the sky
A lonesome man turns wild, grows thinner.
God watches him die.
God is thinking:
You, watch out Vladimir![51]
It was He! it was He, from the onset,—
So no one would know who you were,—

---

[49] **Nevsky Prospect:** A busy avenue in the heart of St. Petersburg.
[50] **On a crag:** Here, Vladimir Mayakovsky compares himself to Prometheus, who was punished by Zeus for bestowing the secret element of fire on mortals and chained to a mountain.
[51] **Vladimir:** Mayakovsky's poetry always reflects his inner self. Therefore, it's not surprising to see the author's name mentioned in the poem.

The Golden-mouthed

It was He, who decided to give you a husband
And placed human notes on the piano board.
If I could tiptoe pass the bedroom door
And make the sign of the cross over your bed,
It would smell of smoldering wool,—
I know,—

And the fumes of the devil would rise overhead.
Instead, until morning, frenzied and nervous,
Thinking that you ran away with a lover,
I rushed all around,
Engraving my cries into verses
Like some madman, — a crazed diamond-cutter.
Oh, to play some cards!
To dip my heart into wine
And to leave it there and allow it soak!

I don't need you!
I don't!
And besides, in some time,
I know
I will surely croak.

If you do exist,
Goodness,
My Savior,
If it's You who have woven the carpet of stars,
If this pain,
That's increasing daily,

Is an ordeal that You've sent down to us,
Then wear the chain of a judge, I pray.
Believe me, I will shortly visit you.
I am punctual
And will not delay for a day.
Listen,
All-highest inquisitor!

I'll shut my mouth.
Not a single wail
Will escape my hard-bitten lips.
Bind me to comets as to horses' tails,
And gallop me,
Tearing my flesh at the stars' bits.
Or else,
When the soul drops the body, decides to leave it,
And comes to your judgment,
Dully flinching,
Then,
Over the Milky Way put up the gibbet,
And like a criminal, seize me and lynch me.
Do what You will,
Quarter me! and let me remain thus.
I myself will wash Your hands clean! I allow it.
Only do this
For me,—
Take away that heinous,
Whom You've made my only and true beloved!

The Golden-mouthed

I crumble miles of streets with extended strides.
Bearing this hell, where can I stray thus?!
What heavenly Hoffman[52] alone at night
Thought of your likeness, accursed and heinous?!

II

Both, the sky,
Which in smoke, forgets that it's blue above,
And the clouds, which like ragged refugees rush,
I'll illumine with the dawn of my final love
Shinning bright like the consumptive's flush.

With happiness, I'll muffle the roar
Of the hoard,
Who have forgotten both, home and comfort.
Listen,
People!
Climb out of the trenches, up to the front,
You can fight it out after.

Even if,
Stumbling and wavering, in blood, like Bacchus,[53]
A drunken battle goes on,—
Even then the words of love aren't outmoded.

---

[52] **Hoffman:** (see note 48 on page 75).
[53] **Bacchus:** Vladimir Mayakovsky uses the Greek God of Wine and Drinking to personify the "drunken battle."

The Golden-mouthed

Dear Germans!
I know
Goethe's Gretchen[54] must
On your quivering lips be encoded.
A Frenchman
Dies, smiling, on a bayonet;
A shot-down pilot crashes with ardor,
If they're able to recollect
The kiss of your lips,
Traviata.[55]
But as for me, I simply don't have the time
For the rosy pulp that the centuries chew on.
Come and embrace new legs tonight!
A redhead,
In makeup,—
I am singing of you now.

Perhaps, from these days,
Horrifying like the bayonet's edge,
When the centuries bleach my beard silver,
Only you
Shall remain unchanged,
And I,—
Following you from city to city.

---

[54] **Gretchen:** The heroine in Goethe's Faust, a symbol of love and purity in German literature. (also see note 22 on page 52).
[55] **Traviata**: ("The Wayward Woman") the heroine of an opera by Giuseppi Verdi, composed in 1853.

The Golden-mouthed

You will be wedded beyond the sea,
In the lair of the darkness, you'll hide,—
Through the London fog, I will kiss tenderly
With the fiery lips of the streetlamps at night.

If your caravan stops in the deserts' expanse,
Where the lions are keen and quick,—
Beneath you,
Under the wind-blown sands,
I will place my Sahara-like burning cheek.

Wearing a smile,
You will see
A fine toreador on the ground!
Suddenly, I
Will fling my jealousy into the crowd
With the bull's dying eye.

If you carry your faltering steps to a bridge,
And wonder
How good it would be beneath,—
It is I,
The Seine[56] flowing under,
Who'll beckon you,
Baring my rotten teeth.

---

[56] **Seine**: A river flowing through Paris, France.

If with another, with the sparks of the hooves,
You light up the Strelka or the Sokol'niki,[57]
Then it is I, tempting you with the moon,
Climbing up higher, naked and calling you.

In the war, they will need someone strong,
Like me,—
They'll command me:
Get killed, cold-blooded!
The last thing I utter,—
Your name shall be
On my shrapnel-torn lip, blood-clotted.

Shall my end be a crown?
Or Saint
Helena?[58]
Now that the storm of life I've tackled,
I'm an equal candidate
For the throne of the universe
And the convict's shackles.

If I'm destined to become a tsar here,—
My men will be told
To imprint your darling face,

---

[57] **Strelka**: An island resort near St. Petersburg, on the Gulf of Finland.
Sokol'niki: A public park in Moscow.
[58] **St. Helena**: an island in the Mediterranean Sea, where Napoleon was detained after the war.

The Golden-mouthed

My dear,
Onto the nation's gold.
But, if I end up there,
Where the tundra swallows the plains,—
Where the North Wind with the river bargains,—
I will scratch Lily's[59] name all over the chains
And kiss them, laboring in the darkness.

Listen you, who forgot the color of the sky above,
Hairy
like animals, wallowing in the slush,
In this world, this is perhaps
The final love
Revealing itself in the consumptive's flush.

III

I'll forget the year, the day, the date.
With a sheet of paper, I'll lock myself up in isolation.
O inhuman magic, create!
Through the suffering words, perform your creation!

Today, just upon walking in,—
Something was wrong in the house,—
I sensed.
In your silky dress, you had something concealed

---

[59] **Lily**: Here, Vladimir Mayakovsky refers to Lily Brik. (see the poem "Lilichka!" on page 23)

And the room smelled strongly of incense.
Are you glad to see me?
A very cold
"very."
Confusion overtook reason and began to fill me.
Burning and feverish, I began despairing.

Listen,
Either way,
You can't hide a corpse.
A terrible lie is lava on the head.
Whatever you do,
Each sinew of yours
Into the megaphone
Trumpets:
I'm dead! dead! dead!
No,
Answer me.
No more lies!
(Where can I go now, disgraced?)
Like two empty graves, your eyes
Excavate two hollows upon your face.

The graves grow deeper.
No bottom at all.
It seems,
I will plunge headfirst from the scaffold.
Like a tightrope, I've stretched out my soul
And juggling words, I totter there, baffled.

I know
That his love is worn out and dull.
Boredom holds you in its captivity.
Reyouth yourself inside my soul
And invite the heart to the body's festivity.

I know
For a woman, every man must pay.
For a while,
I will have to dress you into the gray
Of tobacco smoke,
Instead of the fresh, Parisian style.

My love,
Like an apostle in the time long past,
I'll carry down a thousand thousands roads.
In the ages, a crown for you is cast
And in that crown,
In the rainbow of shudders, shine my words.

As elephants, with hundredweight games, assiduous,
Completed the victory of Pyrrhus,[60]
I packed your brain with the tread of a genius
All in vain.
Nothing could bind us.

---

[60] **Pyrrhus**: According a Greek legend, Pyrrhus was a hero of the Trojan War. The expression "victory of Pyrrhus" means "a costly victory."

The Golden-mouthed

Rejoice,
Rejoice,
My anguish
Is now too great!
You have finished me off!
All I can do is to run to the nearest strait
And thrust my head into the water's maw.

You gave me your lips.
So lifeless they were that my passion ceased.
I froze and pulled back.
It felt as though, repentant, I kissed
A monastery hacked from a frigid rock.

Doors
Banged.
He entered,
Entwined in the streets' delight.
I,
Split in a wail, overflowing with spite.
Cried out to him:
"All right,
I'll go,
All right!
Let her remain.
Dress her up in fine rags,
Shy wings will swell in silk, of course.
Watch out or she'll float away.

The Golden-mouthed

Around her neck, like the weight of a rock,
Tie a necklace of priceless pearls!"

Oh, what a
Night!
I myself tightened the noose of despair.
Seeing me change from somber to jovial,
The face of the room wrenched from the scare.

A redoubling phantom of your likeness arose;
Your eyes illumined the carpet it lied on.
As if a new Byalik[61] had composed
A blinding Queen of the Hebrew Zion.

In anguish,
Before her, whom I had relinquished,
I dropped to my knees, overwhelmingly.
Having surrendered,
King Albert[62], diminished,
Was a gift-laden birthday boy compared to me.

Flowers and grasses, turn gold in the sun!
Turn vernal and lively, o universe!
I desire one poison, just one,—
To keep drinking and drinking this verse.

---

[61] **C. Byalik**: (1873-1934) a Hebrew poet, whose works often dealt with ancient Jewish lore.
[62] **King Albert**: (1875-1934) King Albert I of Belgium during World War I, when Belgium was occupied by the Germans.

You, the thief of my heart,
Who has robbed it of everything,
Into delirium, you've tortured my soul.
This gift, my dear, do not disregard,—
Perhaps, after this, I'll write nothing at all.

Convert into a holiday this precious date!
O, crucifixion-like magic,
Create and create now!
As you see,—
With the nails of words, today,
I am nailed to paper.

1915

I LOVE

Usually So

Love to every infant is given,—
But between work,
Profits
And other stuff,
From evening to evening,
The crust of the heart grows rough.
A heart wears a body,
That body, — a shirt.
And that's not all, they're obsessed!
—An idiot! —
Inventing cufflinks,
Somebody
Started pouring starch all over his chest.
Getting old, they see their mistakes.
The women start creaming.
The men exercise, resembling windmills.

But the skin is already covered with wrinkles
Love gets nourished,
Flourishes,
Blossoms and withers...

As a Kid

As a kid, I was gifted with lots of love.
From childhood on,
Mankind
Is drilled by chores.
But I
Ran away once I had enough,
And procrastinated,
Walking along the Rion[63] shores.
My mom got angry:
"What a wicked child!"
My dad said his belt would teach me some sense.
But I,
With a phony three-ruble bill, lived wild
And gambled with soldiers under a fence.
Without shirts
Or shoes weighing down upon me,
Out, in the sunlight, I sprawled out and baked.
First on my back
And then on my tummy,—
All day long, until my belly began to ache.
The sun was amazed:
"Barely noticeable, there on the shore...
And yet,
Has a heart!

---

[63] **Rion**: a river in Georgia near the village of Baghdadi, Mayakovsky's birthplace.

The Golden-mouthed

The little one knows no bounds!
Where can it have
Enough space to store
Me
The river,
And the towering mountains?!"

As an Adolescent

In adolescence, major decisions are made.
Any fool is taught grammar and reason.
But I
Was kicked out of my school in 5th grade
And thrown in and out of the Moscow prisons.
Your
Apartment-sized world
Is one of the littlest.
There, you breed many curly-haired lyricists.
But who needs those lapdogs, with old, stale lyrics?
I
Was taught
How to love
In the Moscow Butyrkis.[64]
I feel no nostalgia for Bois de Boulogne.[65]
I don't need to sigh when I look at the sea.
By the funeral parlor, sitting alone,
I
Fell in love
With the peep hole of the cell 103.[66]
You see the sun daily,—
You hold it in low esteem,
"What is it worth, that little bright ray?"

---

[64] **Butyrkis:** The Butyrki jail in Moscow, where Mayakovsky served a sentence from 1909-1910 for organizing worker movements.
[65] **Bois de Boulogne:** a well-known public park in Paris, France.
[66] **Cell 103:** The prison cell where Mayakovsky served his sentence.

But if I
Could just catch
A single warm beam,
I'd be willing to give the whole world away.

My University

You know French.
You divide
And multiply even better.
Derive easily?
Well, keep deriving, you hear me?
But tell me,—
Can you sing with the buildings
Together?
Do you know the language that the streetcars are speaking?
As the human fledgling
From the egg first rises,
He reaches for novels and paper to write on.
But I
Learned the alphabet from mass advertisements
Turning the pages of tin and iron.
They take the earth,
Rip it to pieces
And study it,
Stripped,
While the planet itself is tiny!
But I
Learned geography with my ribs
Using the earth as a mattress to lie on.
Illovayskiy[67] is pleading, covered with sweat,

---

[67] **D. I. Ilovayskiy:** (1832-1920) the author of Russian history textbooks.

"Barbarossa's[68] beard – could it really be red?"
Whatever!
This dust-covered rubbish is not worth my worry.
In Moscow, I know every single story now.
They take Dobrolubov[69] (to fight against falsehood),
For even his name
Stands up for the good.
I
Despised the fat ones
Since childhood also,
Always selling my soul to them
For their food.
Here, the gentlemen
Study
So the ladies would like them.
Empty foreheads ring from too much concentration.
But I spoke alone
With the buildings at nighttime,
And with the water reserves
Held long conversations.
The rooftops, listening with every window frame,
Caught whatever I threw into their ears that day

---

[68] **Frederick Barbarossa:** (1123-90), Holy Roman emperor and king of Germany (1152-90), king of Italy (1155-90), and as Frederick III, duke of Swabia (1147-52, 1167-68). The name literally means "red-bearded."

[69] **N. A Dobrolubov:** (1836-1861) radical Russian utilitarian critic who rejected traditional and Romantic literature. The name literally means "the lover of good."

And later,
Their weathercock tongues continued to blabber
About the night
And about each other.

Adulthood

Adults are busy
With bills in each pocket.
Love?
Sure!
For a hundred or so.
But I
Wandered broke,
Homeless
And ragged,
Having no money
And no place to go.
It's night.
You put on your finest faces.
On wives and widows, you practice your moves.
While Moscow
Chokes me in its firm embraces,
With the ring of its endless Sadovaya[70] loops.
In the heart,
Almost clock-like,
The lovers are ticking,
In passionate bedrooms, lighting up with a flare.
But I heard the thundering heartbeats
Of cities,

---

[70] **Sadovaya:** several boulevards in Moscow that come together to form a circle.

The Golden-mouthed

Sprawling across the Strastnoya Square.[71]
My jacket — wide open,
My heart — on the sleeve,
I've opened myself to the sun and the street.
Enter with passion,
Climb into my soul!
My heart is now free! I've lost all control!
In others, I know where the heart has been placed.
Everyone knows that it beats in the chest.
But even anatomy has gone mad in my case,—
Just one massive heart
And there's no room for the rest.
In the last twenty years,
How many springs there,
In my burning and sizzling body, have gathered?
Their weight, still unused, is too much to bare,
And not just in verse,
But in reality, rather.

---

[71] **Strasnaya Square:** A square in Moscow, named after the Monastery of Christ's Passion.

What Became of it

More than allowed
And much more than needed,
As though disillusioned by the poetic fate,
The lump of the heart grew bigger and bigger,
And big was my love,
And big was my hate!
Under that burden,
The feet
Stumbled forward,—
I was always well built, you know—
And yet,
Under the weight of a heart, I walked awkward,
And the breadth of my shoulders swayed to and fro.
I swelled with the milk of verse,—
It wouldn't leave me.
It overflowed me, with no where to run.
And I staggered along,
Overwhelmed by the lyric
Of the world-nursing imagery of Maupassant.[72]

---

[72] **Guy de Maupassant**: (1850-1893), French novelist and short-story writer. Mayakovsky makes a reference to "An Idyll," a short story, in which a mother breastfeeds a hungry peasant boy.

I Call

Like a heavyweight lifter,
I stumbled on, tired.
I called,
As if summoning people to vote,
Or alarming
The villagers
That there's a fire:
"Here!
Here it is!
Help me carry my load!"
When they saw such a bulk sobbing and wailing,
Through the snow
And the mud
Running,
In fright,
All the ladies quickly scurried away from me:
"That's too much…
We just wanted a tango tonight."
I can do it no more,—
And yet, I carry this burden,
I will throw it away,—
But I won't,
That's for certain.
I walked on, enduring the pain in my chest.
My ribcage was trembling under the stress.

You

You came
Attracted
By my roar
And my height,
But looked closer
And saw there, merely a boy.
You
Took my heart away,
Like it was all right,
And went on playing,—
Just a girl with her toy.
And everyone,
Stood there, rather bewildered.
Ladies and maidens
Were gaping at you.
"Love such a fellow?
Why, one day, he'll kill you!
She must be a tamer,
Straight out of the zoo!"
But I felt unyoked,
Triumphant
And proud!
And I was oblivious in my delight!
Like a bride-happy Indian,
I leapt all about.
I felt so elated…
So elated and light.

The Golden-mouthed

Impossible

I can't lift the grand piano,
All on my own,
(And the steel safe
Is also too heavy to do)
But if not the safe
Or the piano,—
Alone,
How could I carry my heart back from you?
The bankers all know:
"In money, we bathe.
If the pockets are full,—
Place it all in the safe."
I've hid
All my love
Into you
Like riches in steel,
And walked on, like Croesus,[73]
But wealthier still.
And,
If desire really demands it,
I'll take out a smile,
Or whatever
The cost,

---

[73] **Croesus:** reigned about 560-546 BC, last king of Lydia, an ancient country of Asia Minor, well-known for his wealth.

And
Party all night
With all of my friends there
Spending some fifteen lyrics, at most.

It's the same with me

Fleets! Even fleets rush to the port.
The train — even the train speeds to the station.
But I'm being pulled to you all the more
For I love you!
And I haven't got patience.
Pushkin's knight[74] goes down into his vault
To marvel and joyfully gape at it all.
It is thus,
I return to you,
My beloved,—
To stare at my heart,
For I know that you'll have it.
When people come home,
They feel happy and free.
They wash their dirty hands and shave,—
Don't you know
It's exactly the same
With me,—
When returning to you,
I come home, all the same.
The earthy man is laid into earth.
In the end, we have to return to our ends.
Thus I
Reach back for you with all of my verve,
Just as soon as we part,
Separating our hands.

---

[74] **Pushkin's Knight:** refers to A. S. Pushkin's play, "The Covetous Knight."

Outcome

Neither miles
Nor quarrels
Can make love perish.
Thought out
And tested
All through.
Raising the sheet of verses,
My cherished,—
I swear that my love is both,
Constant and true.

1922

BORIS PASTERNAK

FEBRUARY

Oh February, to get ink and weep!
To write about it mourning,
While the uprising, raging sleet,
Like in the spring, is burning.

To rent a buggy. For six grivnas,[75]
Ride through the blare of bells and wheels,
Where the persistent rainfall drizzles
Much louder than ink and tears.

Where, like the charcoal pears, the crows
From trees, by thousands, will rise,
Crash into puddles, and then toss
Dry sadness deep into your eyes.

---

[75] **Grivnas:** a Russian coin equal to ten kopecks.

Below, thawed patches glisten through,
With loud cries, the wind is grubbed.
The more haphazard the more true,—
The poems are composed and sobbed.

1912

VENICE

So early that it hadn't dawned,
The ringing windowpanes awoke me.
A moistened pretzel made of stone,—
Beneath me, Venice floated calmly.

Now, all was calm, but all the while,
While still asleep, I heard a cry
And like a mark that had been silenced,
It still disturbed the morning sky.

Scorpio's trident, — there it dangled
Above the mandolins. Perchance,
Somewhere afar, a woman, angered,
Had voiced the call in her defense.

Now it was hushed and in the skyline,
As though a pitchfork, it got stuck.
The Grand Canal, with nervous smiles,
Much like a fugitive, gazed back.

And rushing, hungry and stretched out,
The jaded waves already neared.
The gondolas beat, tightly bound
And honed their noses on the pier.

Beyond the docks of boats, already,
From dreams, reality was raised
And Venice, — a Venetian lady
Was diving off the bank with grace.

1913

AFTER THE INTERLUDE

Three months ago, it all had started.
The early blizzards swept by, rushing
Over our fields and yards unguarded
With some unmanageable passion.

Then I made up my mind at once,—
As though a hermit on vocation,
I'd write of winter and perchance,
I would complete my spring collection.

But trivialities, like mounts, arose,—
Like snow-banks, standing in my way.
My plans and winter intercrossed,
As winter passed on, day by day.

The Golden-mouthed

I, then, perceived and got to know
Why on this foul and stormy night,
She pierced the darkness with the snow
And peeked out of the yard inside.

She sighed and whispered to me tensely,
"Please hurry!" — pale from the cold.
But I was sharpening my pencil
And awkwardly, dismissed her call.

And while one early morning, I,
Behind the desk, delayed each sentence,
The winter came... and passed me by
With some unrecognized resemblance.

1957

NOBEL PRIZE[76]

All is lost, I'm a beast in a pen.
There are people and freedom outside,
But the hunters are already at hand
And I haven't a way to take flight.

The bank of a pond... woods at night
And the trunk of the pine lying bare.
I am trapped and cut off on each side.
Come what comes, I simply don't care.

Am I a murderer, a villain, a creep?
Of what crime do I stand here condemned?
The whole world listens, ready to weep
At my words of my beautiful land.

---

[76] **Nobel Prize**- Boris Pasternak was, in fact, awarded the 1958 Nobel Laureate in Literature for his important achievement both in contemporary lyrical poetry and in the field of the great Russian epic tradition. (Accepted first, later caused by the authorities of his country to decline the prize.)

Even now, at the edge of the tomb,
I believe in the virtuous fate,—
And the spirit of goodness will soon
Overcome all the malice and hate.

1959

PEERLESS DAYS

During the lengthy winter terms,
The days of equinox[77] I've greeted
And each was peerless in its forms
And endlessly each day repeated.

A sequence file made of them,
A bit by bit, would slowly mold,—
Those solitary days, just when
The time completely seems to halt.

And now each day I recollect: —
The winter is halfway completed,
The roofs are leaking, roads are wet,
Upon the ice, the sun is seated.

---

[77] **Equinox**: occurs on March 21st when the sun crosses the equator and day and night are everywhere of equal length.

And lovers reach out to embrace
So eagerly, as if they're dreaming.
High in the trees, from sultry rays,
The starling-houses are steaming.

The restless clock-hands are too tired
To endlessly turn 'round the face
And in a day, decades expire
But nothing ends the warm embrace.

1957

THE POETRY
OF
DR. ZHIVAGO

HAMLET

The clamor ebbed. Appearing on the stage,
I walked ahead and leaned against a jamb.
I listened in the echo's distant range
For what would happen in the age to come.
The twilight of the night has gathered,
Converging all binoculars on me.
If only you are willing, Abba Father,
I beg you, take this cup from me.[78]
I love your plan, so fixed and stubborn,
And I'd agree to play this role,
But as of now, there's another drama,
This time, dismiss me, I implore.

---

[78] **"Take this cup from me..."** In the Agony of the Garden, Jesus prayed, "Father, if You are willing, take this cup away from me. Nevertheless, let your will be done, not mine." (Luke 22:39-44)

But the predestined plot proceeds,
The outcome of my fate's already sealed.
I am alone, all sinks in phariseeism[79]
And life is not a walk across a field.[80]

1946

---

[79] **Phariseeism:** self-righteousness or hypocrisy, especially with regard to adherence to rules and formalities.
[80] **"And life is not a walk across a field..."** A Russian proverb which means that to live a life is not an easy task.

MARCH

The sultry sun heats to the seventh sweat.
The ravine rages in the frenzy, senseless.
As though a cowgirl working in the stead,—
The spring is busy, and its chores are endless.

Out in the light, the snow-banks slowly slump,
Their bloodless, twig-like veins turn paler still.
And from the farmhouse, life is smoking up,
The tines of pitchforks breathe with zest and zeal.

These nights. These days. These days and nights!
The thud of droplets in midday, the spatter
Of dripping icicles, — what wonderful delights!
To hear the sleepless brook's relentless chatter!

The Golden-mouthed

The cow-stead and the stable, — open everything!
Gray pigeons peck the oats out of the snow,
And from the all-creating and enabling,—
From all the dung, fresh air begins to flow...

1946

EASTER

There's still the twilight of the night.
The world's so young in its proceeding,
That countless stars in the sky abide,
And each one, like the day, is bright
And if the Earth could so decide,
She'd sleep through Easter in delight,
Hearing the Psalter reading.

There's still the twilight of the night.
It's far too early. It appears,
That fields eternally subside,
Across the crossroad, to the side,
And till the sunrise and the light,
There is a thousand years.

The naked earth appeared deprived,
It had no clothes to wear
To strike the church bells in the night
Or echo choirs in the air.

The Golden-mouthed

And from the Maundy Thursday night
Right through the Easter Eve,
The water bored the coastal side
And whirlpools heaved.

The forest, naked and exposed,
To celebrate the holy times,
As though in prayer, humbly rose,
In congregated trunks of pines.

And in the city, in one place,
Their gathering commenced.
The naked trees sincerely gaze
Above the Church's fence.

Their eyes are overflowed by rage,
And their concern is heard.
The gardens slowly leave their cage,
The earth shakes wildly in its range,
They're burying the Lord.

A light is seen that dimly glows,
Black kerchiefs and long candle rows,
And weeping eyes—
And suddenly, there's a procession,
Bearing the sacred shroud of Christ
And every birch, with a concession,
Along the entrance subsides.

The Golden-mouthed

They walk around the royal square,
Along the sidewalk's edge.
Into the vestibule with care,
They bring the spring and springtime flair,
A scent of Eucharist in the air
And vernal rage.

And March is tossing snow around
To beggars gathered on Church ground,
As though a person just walked out,
Opened the shrine, took what he found
And gave it all away.

The singing lasts throughout the night.
Once they have wept enough, at last, they
Walk humbly, quietly outside,
Onto the street, under the light,
To read the Psalter or Apostles.

But after midnight, all will quiet,
Hearing the vernal lecture,
That if we wait for just a while,
His death won't last, when we deny it
With holy resurrection.

1946

WHITE NIGHT[81]

A far-off time arises in my memory,
The house in the Petersburg Quarters,
A humble daughter of the modest gentry,
Born in Kursk,[82] you are here taking courses.

You are cute, — you have many admirers.
This white night, it is only us two,
Sprawling out on your windowsill, tireless,
From up high, looking down at the view.

The streetlamps, like gaseous butterflies,
Trembled from the morning's first chills
And the words that I whispered in quiet sighs
Resembled the slumbering hills.

---

[81] **White night:** The phenomenon known as the "White Night" occurs in St. Petersburg, where for a period of about three weeks the sun does not set below the horizon and the sky never gets dark.

[82] **Kursk:** a city in western Russia.

The Golden-mouthed

By some chance, we were caught here together,
By one mystery, in the timid fidelity,
As the landscape beyond the Neva,[83] —
Lands of Petersburg stretching unendingly.

In those distant, impregnable thickets,
On this vernal and pale white night,
The nightingales' thunderous singing
Awoke all the woodlands in sight.

Their song was blaring with emotion,
And those birds in a magical chorus,
Evoked both, passion and commotion,
From the depths of the mesmerized forest.

To those parts, like a barefooted wanderer,
By the fence, the night slowly walked
And behind it, from the windowsill, rambling,
Ran the trail of an overheard talk.

Within an earshot of our conversations,
In the fenced enclosures of the garden,
The apple and the berry trees, with patience,
Put on the sunlight's glowing garments.

---

[83] **Neva:** (see note 1 on page 17)

And trees, like phantoms, seeming white,
By the roadside, gathered in line,
To pay their dues to the receding white night
That has witnessed so much in its time.

1953

SPRING FLOODS

The sunset's lights were dying down.
Across the thickets of the copse,
Toward a distant Ural town,
A man was riding on his horse.

The horse was trembling with spite
And echoing the noisy clatter,
The water ran along its side
And wildly splattered in the gutter.

And when he loosened up the reins
Or slowed the pace, alert with caution,
The water swamped the nearby plains
With loud clamor and commotion.

Somebody laughed, somebody wept,
Stones beat on stones with wrathful fury
And wild, raging whirlpools swept
The stumps of trees ripped out fully.

The sunset's pale blaze was sinking.
Out from the distant charcoal trees,
A nightingale starting singing
His blaring song, which wouldn't cease.

There, where a willow in the distance,
Into the gully, dipped her veil,
Out of the seven oaks, he whistled,
As though the Robber-Nightingale.[84]

O, what misfortune, what foreboding,
Could bring about such a shrill?
And with so many shots exploding,
Whom did he really mean to kill?

It seemed that any moment, he,
A goblin and a wanted man,
Would step out on the road to greet
The frontier posts of partisan.[85]

---

[84] **Robber-Nightingale:** a rowdy criminal from an old, Russian fairy tale, who overcomes mortals with his whistling birdcalls and ferocious animal cries.

[85] **Partisan**: a member of a group that has taken up armed resistance against occupying enemy forces, a resistance fighter.

The Golden-mouthed

The woods, the fields, the earth, the sky
All caught those intermittent strains,
Those equal portions of the pie,
Of madness, sorrow, glee and pain.

1953

CONFESSION

Life has suddenly returned again,
Just as once it strangely went away.
On this ancient street, once more I stand,
Just as then, that distant summer day.

Same old people and the same old worry
And the sunset's fire is still warm,
Just as when, the evening in a hurry
Nailed it swiftly to the stable wall.

Women, in their old and cheap attire
Wear away their shabby shoes at night.
Afterward, upon the roofing iron,
By the rooftops, they are crucified.

Here is one, so wearied and unwilling,
Up the steps beginning to ascend,
Rises from the basement of the building,
Walks across the courtyard on a slant.

The Golden-mouthed

And again, I'm planning my charade,
And again, all's pointless and dull.
And a neighbor, passing through the gate,
Disappears and leaves us all alone.

***

Don't cry. Don't tense your swollen lips,
Don't pack them into creases.
You'll irritate those dried up bits
Of scabs from vernal fevers.
Withdraw you hand, don't touch my chest,
We're wires on high voltage.
To one another, by some chance
We may be thrown by fortune.
The years will pass and you shall wed,
You will forget this love then.
To be a woman, — a great step.
To drive insane, — a talent.
Under the spell of female hands,
Of charming shoulders, backs, and necks,
As you can see, I've lost my sense,
Bewitched by their divine effects.
No matter how the night might bind,
The dismal ring just cannot match
The force by which I'm held confined
And passion tempts me to detach.

1947

SUMMER IN THE CITY

Soft exchanges fill the air
And in some fervent rush,
From the forehead, strands of hair
Were gathered with a brush.

Helmed, she casts a single glance
Upon your face and waits,
Throwing back her head at once
With her dangling braids.

While the humid, muggy night
Insinuates a storm,
All the passersby outside
Quickly scatter home.

The Golden-mouthed

And the thunder can be heard now.
There, resounding, it rings.
By the widow-frame, the curtain,
In the crosswinds, swings.

All is silent, all is hushed now
And it's humid all the while,
And the lightning's golden flashes
Are still groping in the skyline...

But the sunrise will ensue
With a breaking light, so stifling,
And dry the puddled avenues,
From the downpours and lightning.

You will then discern a stagnant,
Wearied look, still quite sedate,
On those age-old and those fragrant
Limes that simply will not fade.

1953

THE WIND

I've ceased to be, but you're alive.
The wind is whimpering and sobbing.
It rocks the forest and the cabin.
At once all of the tree trunks bending,
Not individually each pine,
Over the endless hills extending,
Like bodies of the yachts aligned
Along the coast, a storm withstanding.
And all this not from heedless pride
Or from a pointless, frenzied folly,
But to compose a lullaby
For you in time of melancholy.

1953

HOP[86]

Under the broom, entwined by ivy,
From rain, we're hiding for the time.
A cloak protects our shoulders slightly,
Around you, my arms — entwined.
No, I was wrong. Among these shrubs,
Not ivy, but green hop has widened.
So, should we spread this cloak, perhaps,
Over the grass for us to lie on?

1953

---

[86] **Hop;** the Russian word "*hmel*" has multiple meanings and can be translated into English as "hop" or "intoxication."

INDIAN SUMMER

The currant leaf is prickly and coarse.
The windows in the house ring with laughter.
There, women shred it, peppering the cloves,
And marinate it all soon after.

The forest heaves, like a mocking scoffer,
All of this clamor onto the slope of the hill,
Where the sun-burned hazel hangs over
As though a campfire scorches it still.

Here, the path leads down to the gorge,
Where the snags lie parched and dismantled.
Feeling pity for autumn, you watch
As it sweeps everything down the channel.

And it's sad that the universe's simpler
Than the scholars may like to pretend,
And it's sad that the copses are sinking in,
And that everything's reaching its end.

That it's useless to gawk at it all,
When the valley is burned into cinder
And the pale white soot of the fall
Pulls the gossamer into the window.

The garden fence is broken on the side,
And birches hide the narrow, dusty trail.
There's laughter and hubbub inside,
The same clamor is heard on the vale.

1946

AUTUMN

I've set my folks on a vacation,
From friends I've drifted far apart,
And now the permanent dejection
Submerses nature and the heart.

Inside this lodge, we're left alone.
The woods are dreary and remote.
And sprouts of grass, like in the song,
Have overgrown each path and road.

The lodge's wooden walls now gaze
At us with grief and hopelessness.
We never vowed to break restrains,
We will decline with openness.

We'll sit at one. By three, we'll rise,
I — with my book, you — with the sewing.
There won't be time to realize
How we stop kissing in the morning.

The Golden-mouthed

The leaves, spontaneous and vast,
Will rustle, gliding though the air
To fill the cup of sorrows passed
Once more, with present day despair.

Such zest, affection and delight!
We'll rush into September's riot!
In autumn rustle, come and hide,
Go crazy, or just stand there quiet!

The way you shed your clothes in haste,
Like woods shed leaves onto the ground,
When falling into my embrace,
You fling aside your dressing gown!

You are the boon of a fatal step,
When living life becomes a bother,
And beauty's root is courage and
This draws us closer to each other.

1949

FAIRYTALE

Once upon a time,
Somewhere far away,
Riding through the steppe,
A horseman made his way.

Through the dust, he saw,
While he sped to fight,
A forest was emerging
Dreary, dark and wide.

His soul cried out in worry,
And his heart would race:
Tighten up your saddle,
Fear the watering-place.

But he didn't listen,
And only gaining speed,
Straight onto the mound
He would lead his steed.

The Golden-mouthed

Turning from the barrow,
To an barren vale,
Past the higher ground,
Straight across the dale.

Down into the furrow
He took his horse apace
Where the trail led him
To a watering-place.

Heedless of the warning,
Quick to move, he took
His horse to drink the water
From the hidden brook.

Near the shallow water,
Where he made his way,
Sulfur flames illumined
The entrance to a cave.

In the crimson smoke
That shrouded everything,
With a distant calling
The forest seemed to ring

Straight across the ravine,
Startled and appalled,
The rider walked his horse
To the haunting call.

As he neared, a dragon
Suddenly appeared.
The rider saw its tail
And tightly gripped his spear.

The dragon breathed out fire
With a blinding light,
Thrice around a maiden
Winding his spine.

The body of the dragon,
Bending like a whip,
Held the maiden's shoulder
With a solid grip.

A beautiful, young maiden,
By that county's customs,
Was given to the monster
As a form of ransom.

The Golden-mouthed

The village folk surrendered
This beauty with high hopes
To satisfy the serpent
And protect their homes.

The monster squeezed her arms
And coiling her throat,
He left the victim feeling
Hopeless and distraught.

The rider, with a prayer,
Gazing at the sky,
Ready for the battle,
Held his spear up high.

Eyelids tightly shut.
Summits. Clouded spheres.
Waters. Fords and rivers.
Centuries and years.

The wounded rider lies.
His body barely moves.
The loyal horse is trampling
The dragon with its hooves.

The dragon's body's fallen
By the watering-place.
The rider is a confounded.
The maiden's in a daze.

The midday sky is shinning,
As azure clouds unfurl.
Who is she? A princess?
Or just a peasant girl?

Now, in joyous happiness
The soul can't cease to weep,
And now, unable to resist,
The body falls asleep.

Now, his health's returning
Now, he's weak once more.
From the loss of blood,
He's feeling weak and sore.

But their hearts are beating.
First one, then the other
Coming back to life
And falling back in slumber.

The Golden-mouthed

Eyelids tightly shut.
Summits. Clouded spheres.
Waters. Fords and rivers.
Centuries and years.

1953

AUGUST

As was promised, so it happened,
The morning sun rose rather early.
Its sultry, saffron beam fell slanted
Between the sofa and the curtain.

It covered with its scorching red
The village and the nearby wood,
The dampened pillow and my bed,
The corner where the bookshelf stood.

Then I recalled what had been done
To make my pillow moist, I ached,
I dreamt you walking, one by one,
Across the forest to my wake.

And while the crowd was proceeding,
All of a sudden, someone stirred:
It was the sixth of August, meaning,
— Transfiguration of Our Lord.

The Golden-mouthed

This day, from Mount Thabor, often,
A flameless light burns through the skies
And autumn, like a lucid omen,
Draws to itself observant eyes.

One by one, you rambled, sighing,
Across the trembling grove, ahead
Into the graveyard that was shinning
As though a russet gingerbread.

Up there, upon its silenced tops,
The royal sky was seated proud
And with the crowing of the cocks,
The spacey distances rang out.

There, like a government surveyor,
Stood Death, and with her chilling eyes
Stared at my face, so ghostly pale,
To estimate my casket's size.

All sensed someone, so calm and poised,
And heard his voice from where I lay.
It was my own prophetic voice
That spoke, untouched by the decay:

"Farewell, the blue Transfiguration,
Farewell, the gold of festive blessings.
Come soothe this hopeless desperation
With a woman's gentle, soft caresses.

Farewell, the years and timeless chase.
Farewell, the women who'd confront
The voids of sorrow and disgrace.
I am the field on which you fought.

Farewell, the wingspan and the reach,
Farewell, the free, persistent soaring,
And world's reflection caught in speech,
Creative work and wonder-working."

1953

WINTER NIGHT

The blizzards all across the earth,
Have swept uncurbed.
The candle burned upon the desk,
The candle burned.

As in the summer, moths are drawn
Towards the flame,
The pale snowflakes soared
Towards the pane.

Upon the glass, bright snowy rings
And streaks were churned.
The candle burned upon the desk,
The candle burned.

On the illumined ceiling,
Shadows swayed,
A cross of arms, a cross of legs,
A cross of fate.

And with a loud thud, two boots
Came falling down,
And from the candle, tears of wax
Dripped on the gown.

And nothing in the snowy haze
Could be discerned.
The candle burned upon the desk,
The candle burned.

A gentle draft blew on the flame,
And in temptation,
It raised two wings into a cross
As if an angel.

The blizzards swept all through the month.
It so occurred,
The candle burned upon the desk,
The candle burned...

1946

PARTING

A man out of the courtyard gapes,
Not knowing what to say.
Her leave was much like an escape.
The house is disarrayed.

There's chaos all around the room.
He cannot comprehend,
Because of tears, because of gloom,
The damage's extent.

He hears a ringing in his ears.
Perhaps he's going mad?
How come the notion of the seas
Is growing in his head?

When icy windows block the light
And one can barely see,
The suffocating grief is like
The desserts of the sea.

The Golden-mouthed

He dearly loved all of her traits
And he and she were close,
Like shores are intimate with waves
Along the whole wide coast.

Like rushes, after passing storms,
Can drown in the tide,
So drowned all her features, forms,
Within his soul that night.

In time of conflicts, struggles, when
His life had lost its sense,
The wave of fortune brought her in
To him out of the depths.

Through obstacles, in a frenzied stir,
From hazards they had steered.
These waves had carried, carried her
Until they brought them near.

And now, she suddenly took off.
Yes, she was overpowered!
The parting will consume them both,
By grief, they'll be devoured.

The Golden-mouthed

The man now overlooks the place.
Before she left, she tossed
Out of the cupboard in a haste
Her dresses and her clothes.

He wanders, and until the night,
He folds the stuff she scattered.
Into the drawer on the side,—
Her scrap, her sewing patterns.

Next to her work, he slowly kneels.
The needle's pointing up.
Before him she again appears,
And he begins to sob.

1953

MEETING

The roads will fill with snow,
The roofs will feel its weight,
To stretch, outside I go:
There, by the door, you wait.

Alone, in an autumn coat,
With nothing on your head,
You chew the snow, distraught,
And hide a nervous fret.

The fences and the trees
Into the gloom withdraw.
You stand there in the breeze
Under the falling snow.

The headscarf droplets slide
Along the coat you wear,
As dewy drops alight
And sparkle in your hair.

The Golden-mouthed

A pale lock will trigger
Enough of light to note
The face, the scarf, the figure
And this light, autumn coat.

There's wet snow on your lashes.
Your eyes appear displeased.
Your whole appearance flashes
In one entire piece.

As though a scrap of metal
Into the stibnite dipped,
Across my heart unsettled,
You were incised in script.

And in it, now forever,
Your humble features stay
And thus, it doesn't matter
If life is harsh today.

That's why the night appears thus
Redoubled in the snow,—
No boundaries between us,
And closer still we grow.

But who are we, from where,
If from those years, today,
Just rumors are to spare,
And we've long passed away?

1949

SUNRISE

Sometime ago, You were my life.
Then came the war, the devastation.
You left me all alone, in strife,
Without a trace or explanation.

When many years had passed me by,
Your voice awakened me by chance.
I sat and read Your Word all night
And came to life out of a trance.

Since then, I feel more drawn to people,
To blend into the morning crowd.
I'll cause commotion and upheaval
And send the sinners bowing down.

Outside I rush for this alone.
Like for the first time, standing speechless,
I see these streets and snowy roads,
These desolate, abandoned bridges.

The Golden-mouthed

I'm welcomed everywhere I visit.
There's light and comfort, and time flies.
And in a matter of just minutes,
The city can't be recognized.

The blizzard's weaving by the gate
From falling snow that won't diminish.
In haste, not wanting to be late,
The people leave their meals unfinished.

For all of them, I feel compassion,
As if their troubles are my own.
I melt, myself, like snowflakes ashen,
And knit my brows like the dawn.

I walk among these nameless men.
Before my eyes, the world is spinning!
I feel won over by all of them,
And only in this is my winning.

1947

EARTH

Into the Moscow's manor estate,
Spring barges in, stern and austere.
From opened closets, moths appear
And crawl across the summer gear,
As furs are safely stored away.

And by the window of the loft,
The vernal flowerpots are placed
The gillyflowers bloom with grace,
A sense of freedom fills the place
And dust paves attics gold.

The sightless casement and the street
Are old-time friends each time they meet.
The white night, by the brook, will greet
The setting sun, without a doubt.

And you can hear out in the hall
The stories of the outside world,
Or overhear warm April's call
And eaves respond aloud.
A thousand stories may be told
About the woes of human soul
And though the sunset's growing cold,
It weaves the story out.

Both, eeriness and fire linger,
The same outside as they are indoors.
The air is restless and ferocious.
The selfsame branches of the willow
The selfsame blossoms, white and brittle,
As on the roads, so by the windows,
As on the streets, so in the workshops.

Why then are hills in desolation?
What means this bitter humus stench?
For this then is my true vocation,
So space won't pine in isolation,
So earth won't grieve in separation
Beyond the city's range.

The Golden-mouthed

And every early spring, my friends
Will gather for this reason still.
Our farewell evenings tie loose ends,
Our feasts are merely testaments,
So sorrow, passing through our hands,
May heat existence's chill.

1947

BAD DAYS

When He entered Jerusalem during
The Passion Week, on that day,
Hosannas resounded with fury,
And palm leaves were blocking His way.

But days have grown harsher and crueler
And love, it seems, lost its command.
The eyebrows are frowning rudely,
Here, at last, is the postscript, the end.

As heavy as lead, the grey heavens
Have fallen on top of the roofs.
The Pharisees, shrewd in His presence,
Were secretly searching for proofs.

By the dark command of the Temple,
He was left to a villainous horde.
With passionate hatred, they trembled,
Just as once, they praised Him before.

The Golden-mouthed

The crowds were gathering early
On the neighboring yard, by the gate.
They jostled, awaiting the verdict,
And pushed forth, unable to wait.

The whispers barely reached Him
And the rumors were all on one theme.
His youth and the flight into Egypt,
He remembered it all like a dream.

He remembered the peak he ascended
In the wilderness, and He recalled
The cliff, where Satan would tempt Him
With the kingdoms of the world.

And the wedding at Cana, the feast,
All the wondrous miracles; and
How he walked to the boat through the mist
On the sea, as though walking on land;

And the beggars who met in the hovel,
And the cellar to which he was led,
Where the frightened candle went out
When Lazarus rose from the dead...

1949

MAGDALENE I[87]

Comes night, my demon seems impatient,—
My punishment for past offense.
The memories of dissipation
That drain my heart are still intense.
A slave to men's imagination,
I was a fool who had no sense
And streets were then my habitation.

I'm left with minutes of sensation
Before the somber hush descends,
But in the span of their duration,
Upon the brink, I'll drop, entranced,
My life without hesitation,
As though a jar out of my hands.

---

[87] **Magdalene**: identified as being the unnamed sinful woman who was saved by Jesus and showed her gratitude by washing and anointing His feet on the occasion of Jesus being a guest of a Pharisee. (see Luke 7:36-50)

The Golden-mouthed

Without You, where would I be,
My Savior and my Instructor,
If late at night, eternity
Would not out there to wait for me,
Just like the rookie seemingly,—
A customer that I've attracted.

But, pray, do tell me what is vice,
And sin, and death, and hell, and burning,
When right before their very eyes,
Like trees, we've grafted in our lives
Through my immeasurable yearning?

And Jesus, when Your feet I press
Against my knees, with gentle movements,
I'm only learning to caress
The heavy cross against my chest,
I reach to You and feel so blessed,
Preparing You for the entombment.

1949

MAGDALENE II

The people are preparing for the feast.
Away from the commotion and the stir,
From a bucket resting on my knees,
Carefully, I wash Your feet with myrrh.

There, I grope and cannot find Your sandals,
Tears have blurred my wary gaze.
Covering my eyes, as though a mantle,
Strands of hair have fallen on my face.

I have placed Your feet upon the hem.
Jesus, with my tears I've wet Your legs.
Buried them into my hair. On them,
I have tied the beads right off my neck.

The Golden-mouthed

I foresee the future so detailed,
Just as if You've paused it by my face.
Now, it seems, I'm able to unveil,
Like a sibyl,[88] what will soon take place.

In the temple, veils will fall tomorrow.
We shall gather tightly by the wall.
Under us, the earth will shake with fervor,
Maybe, out of pity for my soul.

Troops will then begin their reformation
And the cavalry will march ahead.
Like a twister in the fury, stationed,
The massive cross will rise up overhead.

By your feet, I'll fall down on the ground.
I will bite my lip and grieve my loss.
Your embracing arms are stretching out
For too many up against the cross.

Just for whom is all of this extent?
All this suffering, this might, these nails?
Oh, how many souls are on this land?
Oh how many cities, rivers, dales?

---

[88] **Sibyl:** a woman prophet or fortune teller.

Before long, three days will come to pass.
They will push me into a regression.
I will wait and finally, at last,
I will come to see the resurrection.

1949

THE GARDEN AT GETHSEMANE[89]

The distant stars were shinning overhead.
Their light was cast upon the curving road.
The road was laid around Mount Olivet.
Somewhere below, the brook, Kedron, had flowed.

The meadow was cut off right in the middle
And there, the Milky Way came into sight.
The grayish olives in their silver glitter
Would try to climb the sky into the night.

In distance, stood a garden. He approached
And leaving His disciples by the wall,
He said to them, "Wait here for Me. Keep watch.
I sense a fatal torment in My soul."

---

[89] **Gethsemane:** olive grove or garden, East of Jerusalem, near the foot of the Mount of Olives. In the Gospels, it is the scene of the agony and betrayal of Jesus. (see Matthew 26:36)

He turned away without exasperation,
As though from what was borrowed in the past,
From both, supremacy and domination,
And now, He was a mortal, just like us.

The widespread darkness now appeared to beckon
Into oblivion, to nothingness, to strife.
The vastness of the universe was vacant,
The Garden was the only place of life.

And looking at these chasms in the sky,
So empty, limitless, He felt a sudden dread.
So that the cup of death would pass Him by
He begged His Father, wet with blood and sweat.

With prayer softening the deadly languor,
He slowly headed back and saw, appalled,
As His disciples, with exhaustion anchored,
Were sleeping on the grass beside the wall.

He woke them up in rage: "Almighty deemed
You worthy of My presence, — you offend Him.
The hour of the Son of Man is here.
Into the hands of sinners, He'll surrender."

The Golden-mouthed

Just as He said this, out of nowhere, stormed
A mob of slaves, and wanderers assembled.
Lights, swords and Judas walking to the front,—
A traitor's kiss upon his lips still trembled.

And Peter gripped his heavy sword. Unsettled,
He cut off someone's ear in the discord.
He hears: "This clash can't be resolved with metal!
Good man, I say to you, put down your sword.

Oh, do you think My Father wouldn't send
The winged legion to protect Me here?
They'd never touch a hair upon My head,—
Without a trace, My foes would disappear.

Know that the book of life has reached that page,
More valuable than all the blessings sent.
What's written in the book cannot be changed,
Then let it all come true, I say. Amen.

You see, My time has reached the final hour.
Continuing, it may alight in gloom.
Thus, in the name of His majestic power,
Accepting agony, I'll step into the tomb.

I'll step into the tomb soon overburdened,
And on the third day, I'll ascent. Into my sight,
As though in a procession for my verdict,
The centuries will flow out of the night.

1949

ACKNOWLEDGEMENTS

I would like to thank everyone who offered me their support while I was working on these translations of Vladimir Mayakovsky and Boris Pasternak.

I am deeply grateful to Jonathan Penton, the editor of "Unlikely Stories" and Max Nemtsov, the editor of "Speaking in Tongues," for publishing some of the early versions of these translations. I would like to thank Vera Zubarev for her kind words of praise and encouragement. I am deeply indebted to Olga Broumas and Rafael Campo for going over the Mayakovsky translations and making some valuable suggestions.

I would especially like to thank my father, Mikhail Kneller, without whom this book would not be possible. Finally, I would like to thank my friends and family for teaching me to believe that nothing is out of my reach.

Andrey Kneller

Printed in the United States
18214LVS00004B/7-24